Land and Estate Management

ACCESS AND OTHER RIGHTS OVER RURAL LAND

Natalie Geen

PACKARD PUBLISHING LIMITED
CHICHESTER

ACCESS AND OTHER RIGHTS OVER RURAL LAND

First published in the United Kingdom, 2021, by Packard Publishing Ltd, 14 Guilden Road, Chichester, West Sussex, PO19 7LA, UK.

This book corresponds to Chapter 11 of the revised fifth edition of *Land and Estate Management,* 2021.

ISBN 978 1 85341 169 4 (paperback only)

A CIP catalogue record of this book is available from the British Library.

Commissioned and prepared for press by Michael Packard.

Front-cover and title page photo courtesy of Carter Jonas

Design and Layout by Hilite Design, Marchwood, Southampton, Hampshire.

Contents

ACKNOWLEDGEMENTS

I would like to thank friends, family, colleagues and tutors who have helped me to obtain the knowledge and experience underpinning this book.

I would also like to thank the Commons.Wikipedia website and the following photographers for the use of their images: Roger Kidd (Figure 1); Derek Harper (Figure 2); Martin Dawes (Figure 3); Andy Scott (Figure 5); Martin vl (Figure 6); and Jim Champion (Figure 7). Figure 4 is my own photograph.

NEG

Figure 1. A farm at Dyffryn Castell, Ceredigion, similar to Fred's, showing a field footpath and overhead electricity cables.

INTRODUCTION

This book focuses on the rights private individuals or public bodies may have, or acquire, over rural land. Knowledge of these rights and their frameworks allows an estate owner or farmer to understand the control others can exert over their land – or conversely the rights they may have over neighbouring land – especially when new rights are proposed or there are disputes over existing rights.

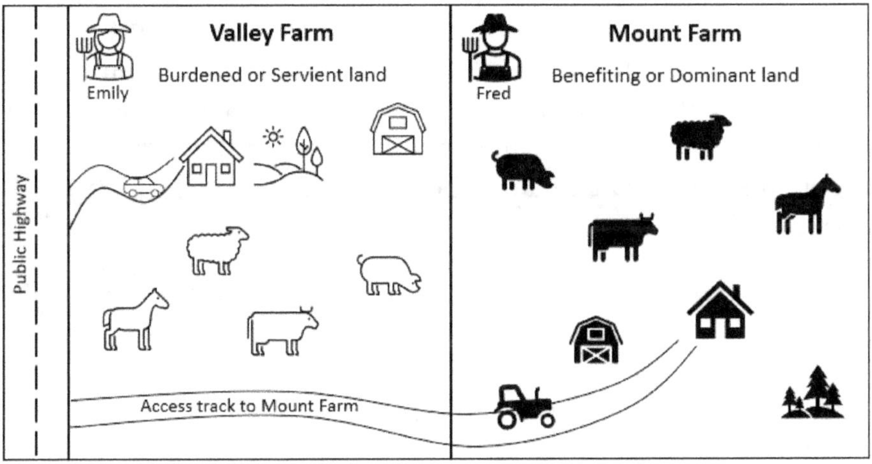

Say Fred owns a 200ha farm. He may have the right largely to manage the land as he wishes. However, consider what happens when there is a public footpath passing through a field; how would that alter his ability to freely manage the field? Consider if there were overhead electricity cables crossing Fred's land; what income would Fred get, and could he get the cables moved if they were inconvenient? Consider when Fred uses an access track over his neighbour's land to gain access to some of his fields; what rights might Fred have to continue using the track if his neighbour objects to his use?

This chapter will cover:

- Rights utility companies may acquire – wayleaves and easements;
- Private rights, such as easements;
- Public rights of access;
- Compulsory purchase;
- Restrictive covenants;
- Registered common land.

It is also worth remembering that, on the sale of land, parties can reserve rights over what they have sold. Perhaps most commonly this is done where there may be valuable mineral or sporting rights. Information on whether these rights have been reserved can usually be found in Land Registry title documents.

GLOSSARY

Before we turn to specific types of rights, it is useful to understand key terminology:

Common Land is land owned by one or several people, but over which other people (commoners) have certain traditional rights, such as for grazing livestock.

Common Rights are the rights which commoners can exercise over registered common land.

Compulsory Purchase is when bodies with certain rights acquire privately owned land, or rights, for schemes of public benefit without the owner's consent, and in return for compensation.

Easements are rights over land which benefit that owned by another party; for instance, a right to cross another's property to access one's own land.

Profit a prendre is a right to go onto another person's land to remove products of natural growth which are usually the property of the landowner, such as wood or wild game.

Public rights are rights that the general public can exercise over land; for example, footpaths and bridleways.

Private rights are rights that private individuals can exercise over land owned by someone else; for example, a right of access to their house.

Prescriptive right is a legal right obtained through long use, usually a period of 20 years.

Restrictive covenants are agreements that restrict one party from doing something. In a lease, a restrictive covenant may prevent a tenant, for example, from using the property for a separate business. In landownership, a restrictive covenant may prevent the landowner from developing land.

Wayleaves are rights acquired when a body with statutory powers, such as a utility company, exercises its powers to install, use and maintain services on, under or over land owned by someone else.

UTILITY COMPANY EASEMENTS AND WAYLEAVES

It is in the interest of wider society to ensure the secure national supply of utility services such as gas, water, electricity and telecommunications. Consequently the Government has granted utility infrastructure providers with statutory powers to acquire rights to install and maintain services routed through land owned by someone else. These powers also limit the landowner's rights to remove the infrastructure to ensure the security and longevity of the services. In return, the landowner or occupier is entitled to claim compensation, which may be in the form of a single one-off or annual payment.

Generally, wayleaves and easements are negotiated with the land owner or occupier to specify and record the rights of each party. Where utility companies require exclusive possession of a site, for example for an electricity substation, a lease governed by the Landlord and Tenant Act 1954 may be negotiated rather than a wayleave or easement. The utility company may also buy the freehold of the land outright in this situation, using their powers of compulsory purchase if necessary.

If a landowner or occupier is approached about the installation of utility infrastructure on their land, they should consider the details of how the proposals will affect them and their land management from installation through to ongoing use and maintenance of the infrastructure. Depending on the nature of the scheme, some or all of the following aspects may apply:

- ***Wayleave payment*:** Sometimes also called a recognition payment, it is designed to compensate the owner and/or occupier for the ongoing presence of the apparatus. It is calculated differently for the various service media (see below) and can depend on the rights granted. These payments are usually expressed per metre for cables and pipes with additional payments for other structures, for example joint boxes or poles.
- ***Mitigation works*:** In order to reduce the impact of the infrastructure, landowners may wish to consider negotiating amendments to the proposal, such as altering the route; for

example, locating poles in hedgerows rather than across agricultural fields, timing the works to minimise crop or soil damage, or routes to avoid archaeological or designated sites.

- ***Access routes*:** Often services will be over a linear route from neighbouring land, so it may be necessary to agree access routes for contractors to the work sites or compounds. Likewise it is important to ensure farm and estate access is maintained, and appropriate temporary access routes are provided through the working areas if necessary.
- ***Compounds*:** Particularly with large-scale infrastructure projects, construction companies can require working compounds on rural land to store materials, machinery, and welfare facilities for employees. Terms for these agreements can often be negotiated separately to the wayleave.
- ***Crop loss*:** If crops are lost or damaged as a result of the installation of the apparatus, the occupier can claim compensation; for example, total crop loss during the installation period and lower yields in the subsequent year.
- ***Basic Payment Scheme (BPS) loss and impact on agri-environment schemes*:** Some works will make land temporarily or permanently ineligible for BPS. Likewise some works may breach terms of an agri-environment scheme and may need the prior approval of the Rural Payments Agency (RPA). The impact of this is likely to alter in coming years as BPS is delinked and phased out and new agri-environmental schemes are introduced.
- ***As-laid plans*:** It can be useful to request as-laid plans as a record of services laid and the routes, particularly for underground infrastructure.
- ***Any extra costs incurred:*** For example, an occupier may incur costs for additional cultivations or working around a site during construction.

- ***Reinstatement costs:*** If there is any damage during the installation works which the utility company has not put right, the owner or occupier may need to claim the costs back from the utility company; for example, rutting from heavy machinery or damage to land-drainage systems.
- ***General disturbance*:** Compensation may be required for any loss or damage as a result of the works; for example, contractors leaving gates open and stock straying.
- ***Injurious affection*** is where the freehold value of land is decreased due to the presence of infrastructure. It is usually only relevant for larger utility schemes, such as high-voltage overhead power lines. Where there is quantifiable development-value, the claimant may also be able to claim further compensation.
- ***Reasonable professional fees*:** In most cases professional – surveyor and legal – fees are reclaimable if a wayleave professional is instructed to act on the owner or occupier's behalf.
- ***Claimant's time and resources*** are usually reclaimable. It is important to keep a detailed diary of management time and resources incurred in dealing with the matter in order to help provide evidence of costs.
- ***Schedule of condition*:** In order to claim some items of compensation, it may be necessary to prove the original condition of the land through an appropriately dated record of condition, ideally agreed with the utility company before it takes entry, and supported with photographs or video evidence.

The sections below briefly consider the frameworks within which each utility sector operates.

Gas

The Gas Act 1986 (as amended by the Gas Act 1995) gives public gas transporters compulsory acquisition rights to lay pipes on private land. However, the statutory process is time-consuming and costly so most rights are acquired by agreement with a landowner and the statutory rights only used as a last resort. If agreement cannot be reached, the Secretary of State may authorise the compulsory purchase of the necessary rights.

In order to install a pipeline, the gas company may need a fenced off 'temporary working strip' which is wider than the easement strip for the access of machinery and sub- and top-soil storage.

Generally the payments to landowners are 80 per cent of the bare agricultural land value of the easement width for a permanent easement. Additional payments for crop loss, damage, disturbance and professional fees may also be made where relevant and proven.

Electricity

The Electricity Act 1989 gives appropriate companies the right to acquire a wayleave to install an electricity line on, under or over private land, together with rights of access for inspection, maintenance and replacement. Electricity companies also have rights to lop trees to protect their apparatus, although they must pay the reasonable costs.

As with gas companies, electricity companies generally prefer to negotiate rights rather than using their statutory powers. However, if the parties do not agree, electricity companies may serve notice on the landowner and, if the landowner continues to refuse consent, the company can apply to the Secretary of State for the grant of rights. Landowners have a right to terminate some electricity wayleaves with a system of notices; however, the electricity company can then opt for a 'necessary wayleave' under the 1989 Act, or a compulsory purchase order.

There are agreed industry-standard rates for electricity wayleave payments. The rates are voluntary and vary depending on the type of apparatus (overhead cables, underground cables, poles, etc.) and the type of land they are situated in (arable, grassland, field margin, etc.). The current rates are available from the National Farmers' Union, Country Landowners' and Business Association or the Farmers' Union of Wales.

Figure 2. An electricity pylon in the rural landscape, near Seale-Hayne, Devon.

Water and sewerage

Water companies have some of the strongest powers of all the utility providers under the Water Industries Act 1991, the Water Resources Act 1991 (as amended by the Environment Act 1995) and the Land Drainage Act 1991. They can serve notice of their intentions and then enter the land, for example to lay a new pipeline, but also to inspect, maintain, repair or alter a pipe. Nevertheless, they must give reasonable notice – usually a minimum of three months. The Environment Agency also has compulsory powers to lay new water and sewerage pipes.

The recognition payment for water pipelines is based on how much the value of the land is depreciated by the presence of the pipe. This is generally taken as half the value of the land area affected with the water company specifying the width. Nevetheless, *St John's College Oxford v. Thames Water (1990)* established the principle of 50 per cent of the value of the full working width. Once the pipeline is installed a landowner may require the water company to remove the pipe if it is reasonable to do so, such as for development of the site. The landowner, however, must meet the reasonable costs of the rerouting.

Telecommunications

The Digital Economy Act 2017 contains a revised Electronic Communications Code, often referred to as 'The Code', which governs the rights of telecommunication operators.

The Code was revised to accommodate the changes that have taken place in technology, government policy and public demand for electronic communications over recent decades. Broadly, it encourages the roll-out of digital infrastructure in order to improve the country's digital connectivity, and strengthens powers for telecommunication operators to install infrastructure on third-party land. This roll-out of digital communications across the country is increasingly affecting rural land.

The Code covers both fixed-line (e.g. fibre) infrastructure and mobile communication infrastructure (e.g. mobile phone masts). If an operator of either type of infrastructure wishes to install apparatus on a third party's land they can serve notice on the landowner and the parties can agree a Code Agreement which grants the operator rights set out in The Code. It is not possible to contract out of many aspects of The Code, so landowners should seek professional advice to ensure their interests are protected as far as possible. If terms are not agreed between the parties within 28 days of a notice, the Operator can apply to the Court to impose a Code Agreement, unless the landowner serves a counter-notice.

The payment for having telecommunication apparatus on land is known as the 'consideration' and is based on the market value of the land, but on the statutory assumption that the site is not being used for electronic communication equipment and that other equally suitable sites are available. This is particularly important for rural areas where a small field corner site may have a relatively low value. Prior to the 2017 Code, landowners could also seek a portion of additional site income when a telecom company shares infrastructure with another such company. This is no longer possible and, in general, considerations for telecom sites have reduced significantly.

The Code is relatively new and is becoming a rapidly evolving and increasingly specialised area, so it is recommended that professional advice is sought and an undertaking for professional fees is obtained from the telecom company.

Figure 3. The Bilsdale transmitting station in Yorkshire; one of the largest in the country, before it caught fire in 2021.

Services in the highway

Highways are treated, by statute, as routes not only for people but also for services for public benefit. Thus the subsoil of a street may be used to carry services without charge, even if it is privately owned. This does not always apply to footpaths or bridleways.

PRIVATE EASEMENTS

We saw above that various utility companies can have rights over privately owned land. Private individuals can also have rights over another's land – known as easements. As we saw in the introduction, Fred could have a right over neighbouring land to access his fields (an access easement). Likewise, a neighbour might have a right to a drainage pipe over Fred's land (a drainage easement). These rights are often recorded on Land Registry title documents.

This section will look at how easements can be identified, created and terminated together with common areas of dispute regarding easements.

Characteristics of easements

The famous land-ownership case in 1955, *Re Ellenborough Park,* held that there were four tests in defining an easement:

- An easement must have benefiting land (known as the dominant land) and burdened land (known as the servient land). Therefore easements attach to the land itself and passes with the purchase or sale of that land.
- An easement must benefit the dominant land. There must be a clear connection between enjoyment of the dominant

land and enjoyment of the easement, such as being able to access property.

- The owners of the dominant and servient land must be different people. (The term 'quasi-easement' is used to describe a right that a person has over their own land.)
- The right must be capable of forming the subject matter of a grant; this means it must be definable (not too vague, like a view), not used and enjoyed jointly with the owner of the servient land, and not involve the servient landowner in expenditure.

Let us consider Fred again. He accesses land he owns at Mount Farm over land owned by Emily at Valley Farm, as shown in the diagram below. Fred's land has the benefit of the access so is the dominant land, and Emily's land has the burden of the right and so is the servient land. There is a clear link between enjoyment of the land and the access and the right which can clearly be defined.

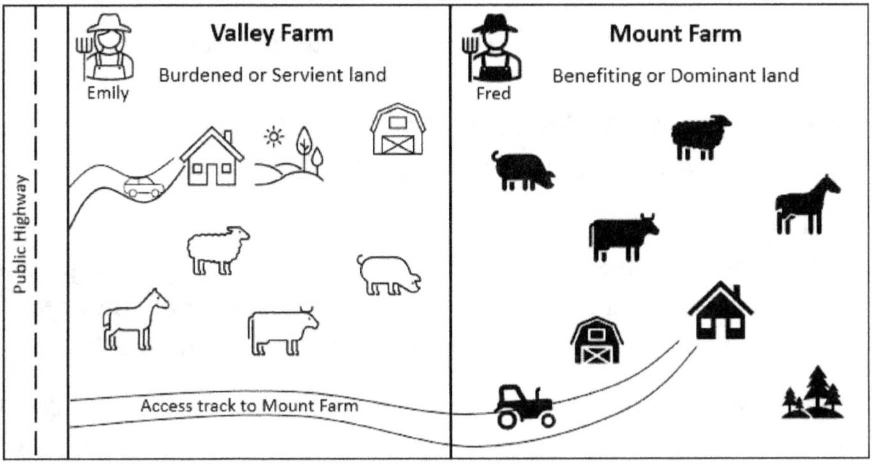

Creating Easements

There are various methods of acquiring easements. The most common are:

Express grant or reservation is where the right is created explicitly and clearly documented. For example, when Emily sold Mount Farm to Fred, there was a clear clause in the conveyance identifying Fred's right of access. Easements can also be reserved by an owner when they sell land. Emily could reserve a right in the conveyance to install drainage over land she sold to Fred in order to benefit Valley Farm. Easements can also be expressly created though a Deed or other legal instrument. In an express easement, the extent of the right is contained in the deed and circumstances when it was made, such as the physical nature of an access route.

Implied grant or reservation is where the right is not expressly documented but is implied through the practices and use of a property, or by the intentions of the parties involved. There are several legal frameworks for implied easements. Broadly speaking, they include 'implied by necessity', for example, when Emily sells Mount Farm to Fred, which is landlocked by Valley Farm, so the only way to access the highway is over Valley Farm; or 'implied by intention' when, say, the septic tank at Mount Farm drains onto Valley Farm land, and Emily intended to give the right to drainage, but it was not expressly documented.

The extent of an implied easement is limited to the prevailing circumstances when it was made; for example, if the land was used for farming where an access easement was created, it would only have been for agricultural purposes.

Long use or prescription is where the right is created by it being used continually, in fee simple and as of right – that is, without force, not secretly and without permission – over the requisite period. There are several legal principles underlying prescription but, broadly, there must be evidence of at least 20 years of enjoyment without interruption or consent must be demonstrated. Under The Prescription Act 1832, 40 years' proven enjoyment can be deemed absolute and indefeasible, unless there was express written consent or agreement to use of the right.

The extent of an easement created by prescription is limited to the use and enjoyment during the prescriptive period. However, an increase in use can rarely be contested, except when it results in a change in the nature of the usage.

Common issues with easements

Difficulties with private easements sometimes arise when either the benefiting landowner is hindered in their use of the right, or the burdened landowner is inconvenienced by an alteration in use of the right.

Where the benefiting landowner, Fred in our example, is hindered in his use of the easement due to Emily's action, for example if she installed and locked gates along the access route, then Fred may have a claim for nuisance. In order to make a successful claim Fred would need to show:

- he was entitled to the benefit of the easement (for example how it was created and that it benefited his land);
- the nature, extent and scope of the easement (often specified in express easements);
- that the interference with the easement was substantial.

Conversely, Emily is not obliged to take positive action, such as track maintenance, to ensure Fred can exercise his right of access (unless the parties have made an express agreement obliging Emily to do so). Fred is, however, entitled to enter Emily's land to carry out track repairs in order to accommodate his right of access. Likewise, where there is a drainage easement, the benefiting landowner is entitled to clear or repair the drains on the burdened land, but must restore the surface of the land to its original condition.

In cases where easements have been created by implication or prescription, disputes can arise over the extent of use of the easement. For example, if Fred developed part of his land, and the access route was used for multiple dwellings, rather than a single farmhouse, Emily might wish to object to the increase in use of the track. When this happens, the change of use is generally deemed excessive if:

- the change in character of the dominant land is radical, as opposed to just intensified;
- the change has led to a substantial increase or alteration in the burden on the servient land.

There has been a variety of court cases on the topic, and it is not always clear whether or not a new use is excessive. When use is excessive, or outwith the restriction in an express easement, the two landowners may renegotiate the terms of the easement, usually in return for a fee to the burdened owner.

Terminating easements

Easements can be released expressly – usually by agreement of the parties – or by implication, for example by abandonment; or if the burdened and benefiting land becomes owned by one person. The express release of an easement must be by Deed to be valid in law.

PUBLIC RIGHTS OF WAY

There is an extensive network of public rights of way through the British countryside which give the public the right to pass over dedicated linear routes. The key classes are footpaths (foot only), bridleways (foot, horses and bicycles), byways open to all traffic (known as BOATs), and restricted byways (introduced by the Countryside and Rights of Way (CROW) Act 2000 as access for all except mechanically propelled vehicles). Under the Wildlife and Countryside Act 1981, county councils have a duty to survey public rights of way within their counties and record them on the Definitive Maps, which are usually available online. Any routes not plotted on the definitive map by 1 January 2026 will cease to have public rights, and it will not be possible to record additional historic ways on the definitive maps.

In addition to public rights of way, some landowners permit public access over specific routes as a permissive rights of way. These do not have to be marked on the Definitive Maps. Where a route is used by permission, even after 20 years of use, it will not amount to dedication of a right of way, so the landowner can withdraw permission should he choose. In order to prevent the unintentional dedication of public rights of way, Section 31 of the Highways Act 1980 enables landowners to lodge maps and statements with their local council to demonstrate their lack of intention to dedicate any further rights of way on their land.

The Countryside and Rights of Way Act 2000 also granted the public the right to wander over mapped open country including mountain, moor, heath, downland (not improved or semi-improved grassland), and registered common land. Eligible land is shown on maps prepared by Natural England and Scottish

Natural Heritage and is reviewed every 10 years. There is no access where there are buildings, golf courses or parks. Access can be excluded for up to 28 days per year. The right is for access only and does not include camping or lighting fires.

Maintenance

The local Highway Authority has a duty to maintain most public rights of way although parish councils can opt to maintain footpaths, bridleways and restricted byways in their area without the prior agreement of the highways authority. Nonetheless, maintenance by parish councils does not absolve local highway authorities from their responsibilities. Likewise in National Parks the National Park Authority may agree with the highways authority to take on maintenance of rights of way.

Maintenance should be sufficient to ensure that the public right of way is capable of accommodating its normal traffic at all times of the year, and should be in keeping with the appearance and character of the surroundings.

Landowners are usually responsible for maintaining gates, stiles and similar structures on footpaths, bridleways and restricted byways. Nevertheless, the highway authorities must contribute not less than a quarter of the expenses reasonably incurred by landowners. If a landowner does not maintain such infrastructure, the highway authority may notify him that it is going to carry out the work, and then recover reasonable costs from the landowner.

If a landowner's trees or other vegetation overhang the right of way so that it impedes or endangers access, the local highway authorities can require the landowner to cut back the offending vegetation. As with stiles and gates, if a local authority has to carry out such work, it may recover costs from the landowner.

Figure 4. A stile on a footpath near the Devil's Dyke, East Sussex.

An occupier of agricultural land has the right to plough or disturb the surface of cross-field footpaths and bridleways. However, they must make sure the route is apparent on the ground to at least the minimum width of 1 metre for a footpath or 2 metres for a bridleway, and is not obstructed by crops. It should be restored to at least the minimum width so it is reasonably convenient to use within 14 day of first being cultivated for a crop, and within 24 hours of any subsequent cultivation. This requirement does not apply to field-edge footpaths or bridleways.

These minimum and maximum widths apply where no width is recorded on the definitive map, and only for the purpose of restoration of highways following disturbance or for keeping them clear of crops. Wherever a width is recorded in the definitive map, the way must be kept clear to that specification.

While not directly related to maintenance of public rights of way, it is important to note the restrictions on keeping dangerous animals in fields with public rights of way. Most commonly in the British countryside this relates to bulls. Bulls can only be kept in fields with a right of way if they are under the age of 10 months or not of a recognized dairy breed – including British Friesian, British Holstein and Ayrshires – and accompanied by cows or heifers. Dangerous animals can also include animals with a known tendency to cause injury or harm, such as dogs or cattle with tendencies to harm people or be aggressive. Likewise dog owners, including people walking with their dogs, have a duty to ensure their animals do not threaten or harm other people. Dog owners are required by law to keep their dogs under close control when on a public right of way. In some circumstances, if a dog is out of control and worrying – attacking or chasing – sheep or other livestock, the landowner may have a legal right to shoot it.

Extinguishment and diversion

If a right of way is problematic, a landowner or occupier can apply to the local authority for it to be extinguished (the public right removed) or diverted. For an extinguishment order, the local authority must be satisfied that the path is not needed for public use, and that it is appropriate for it to be closed. The order must then be publicly advertised and, if any objections are made, the matter is referred to the Secretary of State. It is rare for an extinguishment order to be unopposed and so public rights of way are seldom 'stopped-up'. Even if public rights of way are abandoned, they still require a formal extinguishment order for them to be closed.

Figure 5. The Pennine Bridleway near the Roych, near Chapel-en-le-Frith, Peak District National Park, Derbyshire.

If the right of way seriously interferes with farming, the landowner or occupier can apply for a diversion order. Under the Highways Act 1980, a diversion order may be made if it is required for the efficient use of the land, in the interest of the owner, occupier or general public, and is no less convenient than the existing path. If a diversion takes the route over someone else's land, the landowner may be asked to contribute some or all of the compensation payable to the person across whose land the path will be diverted, as well as any expenses incurred in making up the surface of the new path.

Countryside and Rights of Way (CROW) Act 2000
Under the Countryside and Rights of Way Act 2000 (CROW), the public can walk freely on mapped open countryside (in England and Wales) without having to remain on paths. Open countryside consists of mountain, moorland, heath, downland and registered common land. It does not apply to improved pasture, arable land, parks and gardens unless it has been voluntarily dedicated by its owner for permanent access. It also does not apply to riding horses, bicycles or other mechanical vehicles. Maps of open countryside can be obtained in England from Natural England and from the nature and countryside authorities in the other countries of the UK. Schedule 2 of CROW Act 2000 restricts rights granted under the Act; for instance it gives no greater rights than there are for public rights of way.

Occupiers and landowners have the discretion to suspend or restrict the right of access for up to 28 days each year, for any valid reason. The right also requires dogs to be kept on a lead of no more than 2m length between 1 March and 31 July – the breeding season for ground-nesting birds – or at any time of year near livestock.

Occupier's liability is amended when the public are on land under CROW Act 2000 access rights. The Occupiers Liability Act 1957 does not apply and the Occupiers Liability Act 1984 is reduced so that, unless the occupiers set out to create a risk or are reckless, they own no duty of care for liability for damage or injury caused by natural features, or by people passing over, under or through any wall, fence, gate or stile, except by proper use of those points of entry. This is because the CROW Act 2000 access rights ought not to place an undue burden on landowners and occupiers.

In Scotland, Part 1 of the Land Reform (Scotland) Act 2003 established a similar statutory right of responsible access over most areas of land and inland water in the country.

The foreshore

The foreshore – land that is exposed between high and low water marks – usually belongs to the Crown. Thus public access is technically by permission but is usually provided by custom. The Marine and Coastal Access Act 2009 provided for the establishment of a continuous walking trail around the entire coast of England. Natural England is currently developing this coastal access route, including spreading room between it and the sea. The Wales Coast Path has already been established, making Wales one of the few countries in the World to have a continuous footpath around its entire coastline.

COMPULSORY PURCHASE

Public authorities which need to acquire land to carry out functions which are in the wider public interest have been given powers by Parliament to buy land compulsorily if the landowner is unwilling to sell. This is known as Compulsory Purchase. In practice, the greatest users of compulsory purchasing powers are local authorities and the Highways Agency, although other statutory bodies, such as government departments and utility companies, can also obtain land compulsorily. In theory, an authority should attempt to procure the land by agreement before acquiring by compulsion, but this tends to be easier for comprehensive redevelopment schemes than for linear infrastructure projects through the countryside like new roads and railways, including HS2

Figure 6. The south portal of the A3 tunnel at Hindhead, Surrey – a significant compulsory purchase scheme.

All interests in land can be compulsorily acquired if they are defined in the Compulsory Purchase Order (CPO). This includes freehold interests and any leases or tenancies on the land. Easements and private rights of way are usually extinguished and parties with the benefit of such rights should be entitled to compensation.

Certain types of land are protected from compulsory purchase, including what is owned by the Crown, some National Trust properties, commons and open spaces, and that belonging to statutory undertakers and local authorities. In most of these cases the approval of Parliament itself is needed before compulsory purchase can be commenced, sometimes on the basis that replacement land will be made available, for example where common land is expropriated.

Supposing Mount Farm, in our example with landowner Fred, was on the route of HS2, it is likely that he would have some land compulsorily acquired which would have an impact on his remaining land and farming operations. This section outlines the process Fred would face and the compensation to which he might be entitled.

Process

There are a series of stages in the compulsory purchasing process which the acquiring authority must follow before making a Compulsory Purchase Order (CPO). These include identifying the land required for the scheme and drawing up a schedule of everyone with a legal interest, or right to occupy, in the land to be obtained. The acquiring authority may serve 'requisition for information' forms to help gather this information. The Draft Order must be publicised and the acquiring authority must serve notice on everyone in the schedule, except tenants of one month or less. Therefore Fred, and any of his longer-term tenants, would have notice served directly on them.

Anyone who wants to object to the order can do so in writing to the relevant Government Minister or Welsh Assembly Government within the period specified in the notice, often 21 days from the first notice. Objections may be made by third parties as well as by those with an interest in the land.

If no objections are made and the Minister is satisfied that the proper procedures have been followed, he will consider the case and may confirm, modify or reject the CPO without a hearing. However, if there are 'Remaining Statutory Objectors', that is qualifying people who have an interest in the land or a right to claim compensation, and who have not withdrawn their objections, the Minister is obliged to hold an inquiry, at which Remaining Objectors have the right to be heard. This may be a public local inquiry or, when all the remaining objectors agree, by written representations. Usually, prior to the inquiry the acquiring authority seeks to negotiate with objectors.

Following the confirmation of a CPO, the acquiring authority may purchase the land:

- By agreement;
- Following a Notice to Treat or a Notice of Entry;
- By a General Vesting Declaration (GVD);
- By procedures for acquiring 'short tenancies';
- In response to a Blight Notice.

Notice to Treat is perhaps the most common method when agreement has not been reached. This notice must be served within three years of the confirmation of the CPO and contain a description of the land, request particulars of the recipient's interest and rights in the land, and any claim for compensation; also it must state that the authority is willing to treat (negotiate) for the purchase of the land.

There are other procedures available to acquiring authorities in certain circumstances. For example, Development Consent Orders are used in place of CPOs for Nationally Significant Infrastructure Projects, and Transport and Works Orders are used for developments, such as new railway lines, under the Transport and Works Act 1992. The hybrid parliamentary bill procedure continues to be used for very large and substantial projects, most notably HS2. One reason for its continued use is that there is no scope for a legal challenge once the Act has been confirmed, whereas all the other methods of authorising acquisition allow a short period after ministerial confirmation to challenge the order on legal grounds; for example, in cases when appropriate procedures were not followed, the decision was irrational or people were not treated fairly.

Although there can be very important differences in detail between the different approaches, the broad principles are very similar. The people most affected are warned of what is afoot, and are given the opportunity to make their case before confirmation of the land that will be taken.

Compensation

A landowner may be entitled to compensation when freehold or leased land is acquired, or where no land is taken but his land reduces in value due to the use of the CPO scheme (e.g. proximity to HS2).

The statutory basis for assessing compensation is set out in several Acts, including The Compulsory Purchase Act 1965 and the Land Compensation Acts of 1961 and 1973. It is also supplemented by a large number of case examples. Together they form what is known as 'The Compensation Code'. The underlying principle is that of 'equivalence', meaning that the landowner should be in no worse a position than had the scheme not occurred. The basis of The Code appears in the Land Compensation Act 1965, which gives six rules:

1) No allowance is to be made because the acquisition is compulsory; it assumes a willing buyer and a willing seller. Therefore any increase or decrease in value due to the scheme underlying the acquisition should be disregarded.
2) The value is based on open-market value, assuming a willing seller. So a farm holding could be 'lotted' and development potential can be included.
3) Any special suitability of the land for the statutory use should be disregarded.
4) Any increase in value due to a use which is contrary to the law should be disregarded.
5) Only special cases, such as churches, can be calculated on the costs of equivalent reinstatement.
6) Rule 2 is not to affect assessment of compensation for disturbance matters which are not based on the value of the land.

Let us assume 2ha of Fred's land is to be compulsorily acquired. The items he may need to consider for a compensation claim are:

- ***Value of land taken***: The purchase price for the 2ha of taken land (or other interest acquired) is appraised on the basis of open-market value, disregarding the scheme involved (known as a 'no scheme world'). If Fred had leased out the 2ha, the price paid to him as landlord for land occupied by a sitting tenant would reflect the prospects that he had of regaining vacant possession in the absence of the CPO.

- ***Injurious affection and severance of land not taken***: Injurious affection is the depreciation of retained land as a result of the construction and use of the scheme – the reduction in value of Fred's remaining land. Severance arises from the fact that some land is taken from a larger land holding, rendering it less valuable because it has become too small or an awkward shape. Severance is at its most obvious where land previously held within one boundary ('ring-fenced') is divided into two separate parcels. It is important to note that any compulsory purchase where only part of the land is taken leads to severance. Compensation for severance and injurious affection may be calculated on the basis of either a before-and-after valuation or by adding the value of the land taken to the decrease in value of the retained land. This can also take into account betterment where the value of retained land might increase as a result of the scheme.

- ***Disturbance*** involves the costs and losses incurred as a result of compulsory acquisition, such as the loss of crops and damage from dust. It is important to agree a schedule of condition when the acquiring authority takes entry, and to keep a diary of any incidents and time spent on the compulsory purchase.

- ***Basic loss and occupier's loss payments***: The Basic Loss Payment is to reflect inconvenience and disruption of land being taken. It may be split into an owner's and an occupier's payment.

- ***Accommodation works*** are works carried out on the claimant's retained land in mitigation of a claim for injurious affection. There is no right to accommodation works but they are usually negotiable. They may include replacing hedges, noise insulation or access to severed land.

- ***Professional fees*** may be reimbursed as part of the compensation claim, if they are necessarily and reasonably incurred.
- ***Interest on compensation*** (if relevant) for compulsory acquisition is payable from the date of entry. The Lands Tribunal can also order interest to be paid on its awards.

When part of an agricultural holding is acquired, such as 2ha of Fred's land, Section 8 of the Compulsory Purchase Act 1965 provides a mechanism whereby Fred, in certain circumstances, could require the acquiring authority to purchase the whole holding.

In limited circumstances there can also be a right to compensation for the reduction in value of land caused by the construction or use of the scheme when no land is taken. There are various tests and rules applied to such claims and it is usually deemed preferable, from the perspective of compensation, to have land taken.

The acquiring authority may only take possession of the land once the compensation has been agreed or settled by the Upper Tribunal (Lands Chamber), or when a notice of entry has been served.

In some situations the landowner or occupier may be able to negotiate licences to the acquiring authority for auxiliary works, such as locating a compound on their land.

RESTRICTIVE COVENANTS

We have seen that third parties can have rights to do something on, or acquire, land owned by someone else. Restrictive covenants form a different type of right over land whereby a third party can prevent the landowner doing something on land they own. For example, Emily may hold a restrictive covenant over Fred's land preventing him from constructing new buildings on his land. In effect a restrictive, or negative, covenant is a type of contract between Fred and Emily in which Fred has promised not to do something on his land which will benefit Emily. The covenantor (Fred) carries the burden of the covenant, whereas the covenantee (Emily) receives the benefit. Restrictive covenants attach to land rather than individuals, so if Emily was to sell her land the new owners of her land would continue to benefit from the covenant.

Restrictive covenants may contain various restrictions such as preventing buildings exceeding a certain height – important in the vicinity of airports – and the running of certain businesses or, commonly, the development of land. Covenants are specific to individual properties or parcels of land and are often made when land is sold and the seller wishes to restrict future land uses on the sold land. They are registered in property Deeds and at Her Majesty's Land Registry (HMLR).

If land is subject to a restrictive covenant and the owner wishes to carry out work that engages the covenant, he must seek the consent of the person or body which holds the covenant. In our example above, if Fred wanted to build a new farming building he would have to seek Emily's consent. Depending on the covenant, Emily might grant consent outright, grant consent with conditions (or in return for a fee) or refuse consent.

If work is done that breaches a covenant, the usual remedy is an injunction to stop the activity. Despite this, damages or compensation are sometimes awarded at the discretion of the courts.

The law relating to covenants is complex and legal issues generally focus on whether the covenant is enforceable or if it has been breached. Broadly speaking, restrictive covenants attach to the land and bind what successive owners can do on, or with, the land if the burden:

- is restrictive;
- if the covenantee retains land capable of being benefited;
- if the parties intended that the covenant should run; and
- that the covenant is registered at HMLR (if the land itself is registered).

The benefit:

- touches and concerns the land of the covenantee; and
- the benefit has passed to the successor through annexation, assignment or under a scheme of development.

There are some exceptions to the requirement that the covenantee must retain land capable of being benefited, most notably concerning local authorities and the National Trust who, by statute, can enforce restrictive covenants despite the absence of any retained land.

Positive covenants require an action or payment (such as to keep a boundary in good condition) and usually do not run with the land as the courts have held it would be unfair to bind someone to an agreement to which they were not party.

In some circumstances restrictive covenants can be discharged and becomes unenforceable, for example if there is:

- A change in character of the neighbourhood, so there is no value or benefit left in the covenant;
- An implied or express release of the covenant;
- The burdened and benefited land become owned by the same person;
- An acquisition of the covenant under compulsory purchase;
- A discharge or modification of the covenant by the courts, in practice the Upper Tribunal Lands Chamber, which can vary or modify a covenant and order the payment of compensation where appropriate.

There are proposals, which are not yet implemented, to introduce a new statutory scheme of conservation covenants in England and Wales, which could contain both restrictive and positive obligations for the public good (conservation covenants do not currently exist in the law of England and Wales). The benefits of these covenants are likely to be held by a small group of approved organisations, and they will be available in perpetuity or for a fixed period.

COMMON LAND AND COMMON RIGHTS

Historically common land was unenclosed and unbuilt upon, and was owned by the Lord of the Manor who granted rights over the common to 'commoners'. While much common land was enclosed and lost during the sixteenth century there remain significant commons across England and Wales to this day.

Commons nowadays can be owned by private individuals, local authorities or bodies like the National Trust, but the rights often remain, whether they are used or not. Common rights are often attached to the occupation of a particular property close to a common. Unlike enclosed land, it is the responsibility of neighbouring landowners to fence their land out of the common, rather than vice versa. There are various rights of common:

- Rights of pasture: the right to graze livestock often for specific types and numbers of stock;
- Rights of estover: the right to cut and take wood, reeds, heather and bracken;
- Rights of pannage: the right to turn out pigs;
- Rights of turbary: the right to dig turf or peat for fuel;
- Rights in the soil: the right to take sand, gravel, stone, coal and other minerals;
- Rights of piscary: the right to take fish.

If Fred owned land which was designated as 'registered common', and Emily had a registered right of pasture, then Fred could still use the common for grazing his animals, though he would have to leave sufficient resource for Emily, and any other commoners. Local county, district or unitary councils usually hold the register of commons and rights of common in their areas.

The Commons Act 2006 modernised common land legislation and enabled commons to be managed more sustainably by commoners and landowners working together through commons councils. It also prevents the separation of common rights from the property to which they are attached. In effect, this prohibits commoners from selling, or long-term leasing, rights separately to the property. The 2006 Act

Figure 7. Pannage: pigs grazing here on the New Forest Commons in Hampshire.

attempted to rectify a difficulty in the Commons Registration Act 1965 by giving a second opportunity, in certain circumstances, for land that was not registered as common land under the 1965 Act to be reconsidered for registration. However, the 2006 Act has not been uniformly implemented throughout England and Wales, and some areas still remain under the previous Commons Registration Act 1965.

Common land should remain unenclosed, open and accessible to the public, so the works that can take place on registered common land are very restricted. Any works that may impede or prevent access, such as fencing, buildings or ditches, or which create a new solid surface (such as for a car park) require the consent of HM Planning Inspectorate through a specific common application process.

CONCLUSION

This short book has provided an overview of the main rights a third party can exercise over land owned by someone else, and which are commonly encountered on a rural estate. It has shown that freehold ownership does not always confer a right to do whatever the owner may wish on their land. As such, freehold ownership can also come with obligations or requirements to permit others access to, or forms of control over, the land. In our example, Fred may own Mount Farm but his free management of the land and buildings could be restricted by a plethora of rights other people or companies can exercise, for example:

- Overhead electricity cables may give an electricity company the right to lop trees to protect the electricity network;
- Underground gas pipes may restrict Fred installing buildings in certain locations;
- Neighbours may have private rights to cross Mount Farm to access their land, or for a septic tank soak-away;
- Fred may only be able to access some of his land by crossing neighbours' fields;
- Public rights of way could limit in which fields Fred can keep certain animals;
- Parts of Mount Farm could be compulsorily purchased for a public-benefit scheme;
- A neighbour may hold restrictive covenants over Mount Farm limiting what buildings Fred can erect, in addition to any planning restrictions;
- Mount Farm may benefit from rights of common to graze animals on a nearby Registered Common;

- The mineral rights under Mount Farm may have been retained by a previous owner, giving them the right to enter the farm and extract valuable minerals;
- The sporting or shooting rights may have been sold or leased separately to the land and thus prohibit Fred from shooting on Mount Farm;
- As is demonstrated in other chapters, the land and buildings may also have been let to third parties, sometimes generations ago, further restricting Fred's use of Mount Farm.

The material here is only an introduction and many of the areas can touch on complex legal issues, especially where disputes arise. A full knowledge of the issues can only be obtained by a deeper understanding of land law and the many statutes, regulations and court cases that make up the legal frameworks.

This is also a changing area of law. The Law Commission has specifically reviewed the law of easements and covenants and made recommendations to modernise and simplify the law. These recommendations have not yet been implemented by government at the time of writing, but it should be understood that the following changes are likely in the future:

- To make it possible for the benefit and burden of positive obligations, such as covenants, to be enforced by and against subsequent owners;
- To simplify and make clearer the rules relating to the acquisition of easements by prescription, or long use, as well as the termination of easements by abandonment;
- To facilitate the creation of easements that allow a substantial use of land by the benefiting owner, for example, rights to park a car;

- To expand the jurisdiction of the Lands Chamber of the Upper Tribunal to allow for the discharge and modification of easements.

FURTHER READING

Websites

Common land

Government guidance on works on Common Land: www.gov.uk/government/collections/common-land-guidance

Government guidance on managing Common Land including how to find out if land is registered common land: www.gov.uk/guidance/managing-common-land

Compulsory purchase

A series of government published booklets explaining how the compulsory purchase system works: www.gov.uk/government/collections/compulsory-purchase-system-guidance

Covenants

Government guidance on how to apply to discharge or modify a restrictive covenant: www.gov.uk/guidance/managing-common-land

Easements

HM Land Registry guidance on private easements: www.gov.uk/government/publications/easements/practice-guide-62-easements

HM Land Registry guidance on prescriptive (long use) easements: www.gov.uk/government/publications/easements

-claimed-by-prescription/practice-guide-52-easements-claimed-by-prescription

Further information on the Law Commission review of easements and covenants www.lawcom.gov.uk/project/easements-covenants-and-profits-a-prendre/

General

General information on historical rights that may affect land: www.gov.uk/government/publications/historical-rights-that-could-affect-your-property/historical-rights

Public rights of way

Government guidance for landowners on public rights of way: www.gov.uk/guidance/public-rights-of-way-landowner-responsibilities

Textbooks

Card, R., Murdoch, J. and Murdoch, S. (2005) *Estate Management Law,* 6th Edition. Oxford University Press, Oxford.

CLA Advisory Handbook – CLA82 (2018) *A Guide to the Electronic Communications Code.* Country Landowners' Association, London.

Gardner, S. and MacKenzie, E. (2018) *An Introduction to Land Law,* 4th Edition. Bloomsbury, Oxford.

Moody, J. and Millard, N. (2021) *Agricultural Valuations: A Practical Guide,* 5th Edition. Routledge, Abingdon.

Rodgers, C. (2016) *Agricultural Law,* 4th Edition. Bloomsbury Professional, Haywards Heath.

Sydenham, A., Monnington, B. and Pym, A. (2002) *Essential Law for Landowners and Farmers.* Blackwell, Oxford.

Index

About the Author

Natalie Geen
MRICS, PGDip Surv, BSc

Natalie is a practising Chartered Surveyor with experience in agriculture, rural estate management and conservation land management having worked in practical agricultural roles in the UK and overseas, agricultural research and surveying. She has a BSc (first-class) in Agricultural and Rural Resource Management from the University of Newcastle-upon-Tyne and a post-graduate diploma (distinction) in surveying from the College of Estate Management, Reading.

She is an assessor for the Royal Institution of Chartered Surveyors and has tutored for the College of Estate Management.

Natalie is revising several chapters for the fifth edition of the successful introductory textbook, *Land and Estate Management*, from which this short book is derived.

www.ingramcontent.com/pod-product-compliance
Lightning Source LLC
LaVergne TN
LVHW022031200926
848481LV00007B/2636
* 9 7 8 1 8 5 3 4 1 1 6 9 4 *